Living Fully While We Wait To Die

MINDFULNESS AMID MORTALITY

GEORGE J HATCHER

Introduction

Why do we spend so much of our lives preparing for the inevitable, rather than fully embracing each moment as it comes? This question has lingered with me for years, becoming more urgent as I've crossed the threshold of my seventies. The awareness of our mortality, the ever-present countdown we all share, has both unsettled me and inspired a deeper exploration of how to live fully, even as we acknowledge our finite existence.

Living Fully While We Wait To Die emerged from my own journey through this question. Over the years, I've encountered profound stories of loss and resilience, particularly in my work with families of victims grappling with sudden tragedy in airlline crashes. These encounters have pressed upon me the sense of urgency and importance in living life with intention, mindfulness, and appreciation for the simple, everyday moments that often go unnoticed.

This book is an invitation to explore how mindfulness and presence can transform our relationship with life and death. It's about embracing the impermanence with a spirit of exploration

INTRODUCTION

and gratitude, finding depth and meaning in the time we have. My hope is that in sharing these reflections and insights, you too might find ways to enrich your journey, celebrating each moment as it unfolds.

As you read this, know that a second installment is on the horizon. The next chapter of this exploration will dive into the possibilities of extended life, the ethical and societal questions it raises, and how these emerging realities intersect with our search for meaning. Our shared journey doesn't end with understanding mortality; it expands into the exciting and challenging potential future of human life.

Also By George Hatcher

Mario 1: Woman in Jeopardy

Mario 2: Coming of Age

Mario 3: Risky Business

Mario 4: Free Fall

Mario 5: Afire

Mario 6: Marked

Mario 7: Aftershock

Mario 8: Captivated

Single Titles

One Wilshire

Gabi

Rico

Cats: Meow Is The Language Of Love

HER: Artistic Expressions Through AI

Elegance In White: Through Wedding Gowns

Quinceañera Fashion: Fifteen & Fabulous

Billion Dollar Rainmaker Part I

Pages of Passion Book 1: My First 19 Years

Pages of Passion Book 2: Bold Beginnings

Pages of Passion Book 3: Rising Waves

Pages of Passion Book 4: Threads Of Destiny

Coming Soon

Pages of Passion Book 4: Threads Of Destiny

Pages of Passion Book 5

Pages of Passion Book 6

Pages of Passion Book 7

Mario 9

Gabi 2

Rico 2

Dedication

Molly,

In the dance of life, you are my steady partner,

and in every melody, you are my cherished harmony.

With enduring love,

George

This book can be purchased at over 40,000 bookstores and libraries including brick and mortar stores, online, in print and digital, including Apple, Kindle, and Audible formats. Casa Hatcher Press is a subsidiary of Pretty Face, Inc.

Casa Hatcher Press. http://casahatcherpress.com (800) 416-6189

Copyright © 2025 by George Hatcher. All rights reserved. Printed in the United States of America and abroad.

No part of this book may be used in any manner except in the case of brief quotations in critical articles or reviews.

Book and cover designed by Casa Hatcher Press

Living Fully While We Wait To Die: Mindfulness Amid Mortality by George J. Hatcher

ISBN: 979-8-9989967-8-8 (Paperback)

ISBN: 979-8-9989967-9-5 (eBook)

Living Fully While Waiting To Die

MINDFULNESS AMID MORTALITY

Embracing Our Impermanence

Embracing our impermanence is a profound yet often daunting concept. In a world that prizes permanence and stability, acknowledging that our time here is finite can bring a wave of discomfort. Yet, this discomfort can serve as a catalyst for deeper understanding and appreciation of life. When we accept that every moment is fleeting, we can begin to shift our focus from merely surviving to truly living. Instead of viewing our mortality as a shadow looming over us, we can embrace it as a reminder to cherish the present.

As we grow older, the ticking clock becomes more pronounced. Each birthday serves as a reminder of the years that have passed and those that remain. This realization can incite anxiety, leading us to fixate on what we have yet to accomplish or the dreams we have yet to fulfill. However, this fixation can blind us to the beauty of the journey itself. By reframing our perspective, we can see that our limitations are not shackles, but rather invitations to engage more fully in the lives we lead today. Every interaction, every moment of joy, and even the challenges we face can gain new significance when viewed through the lens of impermanence.

Embracing our impermanence also encourages us to foster deeper connections with others. When we recognize that our time together is limited, we are more likely to express our feelings, share our experiences, and create lasting memories. This sense of urgency can motivate us to reach out to loved ones, to forgive past grievances, and to celebrate each other's presence. In doing so, we create a tapestry of relationships enriched by authenticity and vulnerability, which can nourish our souls as we navigate the complexities of life.

Moreover, understanding the transient nature of our existence can lead to a greater appreciation for the simple pleasures that surround us. The warmth of the sun on our skin, the sound of laughter shared with friends, or the quiet moments of reflection become treasures worth savoring. By cultivating mindfulness, we can anchor ourselves in the present, finding joy in the ordinary. This practice not only alleviates the weight of our mortality but also enhances our capacity to experience life in its fullest form. Each day becomes an opportunity to celebrate the here and now, rather than a countdown to an uncertain end.

Ultimately, embracing our impermanence is not about resignation but about liberation. It allows us to live with intention, purpose, and passion. When we accept that life is a series of moments, each one precious and unique, we can shift our focus from fear of the end to gratitude for the journey. In this way, we can find peace in the knowledge that while our time may be limited, the impact we leave behind and the memories we create can ripple through time, enriching the lives of those who follow.

The Fear of the Unknown

The fear of the unknown is a universal experience, one that grows more pronounced as we age. As we move through life, the inevitability of death looms ever larger on the horizon. This awareness can create a sense of urgency, prompting us to confront our mortality in ways that can be both unsettling and enlightening. Many people find themselves wrestling with questions that have no clear answers: How will I leave this world? What will happen to my loved ones when I'm gone? These uncertainties can lead to anxiety, as the unknown becomes a shadow that darkens our daily lives, stealing moments of joy and peace.

The older we become, the more we tend to reflect on our lives and the choices we've made. This introspection can be a double-edged sword; while it may bring clarity and insight, it can also amplify the fear of what lies ahead. Time feels limited, and the realization that we are all on borrowed time can foster a sense of urgency that drives us to seek meaning in our existence. In this pursuit, we may find ourselves grappling with the unknown in a way that feels overwhelming, as if we are racing against an unseen clock that ticks louder with each passing year.

The fear of the unknown is often rooted in the stories we tell ourselves. We may imagine worst-case scenarios, projecting our anxieties onto our future. This mental narrative can become a prison, trapping us in a cycle of worry and dread. We envision our last moments as filled with pain or loneliness, and these thoughts can prevent us from fully engaging with our present. Instead of savoring the beauty of our daily experiences, we become fixated on an ending that we cannot control. This fixation can rob us of the joy that life has to offer, leaving us feeling as if we are merely waiting for the inevitable.

However, acknowledging the fear of the unknown can also be a powerful catalyst for change. By confronting this fear, we can learn to embrace the uncertainties of life rather than allowing them to paralyze us. We can choose to focus on what we can control—our actions, our relationships, and our perspectives. This shift in mindset can empower us to live more fully, appreciating each moment as a gift rather than a countdown to an endpoint. When we accept that uncertainty is an inherent part of life, we may find that it opens the door to new possibilities and experiences that we would have otherwise overlooked.

Ultimately, the fear of the unknown reminds us of our shared humanity. We are all in this together, navigating the complexities of existence and the shadows of our mortality. By acknowledging our fears and supporting one another in this journey, we can foster a sense of connection and community. Instead of allowing the fear of the unknown to dictate our lives, we can choose to live with intention and purpose, cherishing the time we have while we wait for the unseen countdown to conclude. In this way, we transform our fear into a source of strength, pushing us to live more deeply and authentically in each fleeting moment.

Shifting Perspectives on Death

As we journey through life, the inevitability of death sits like a shadow, an ever-present companion that shapes our thoughts, actions, and emotions. The societal perception of death has evolved over centuries, shifting from a natural part of life to a subject often cloaked in fear and avoidance. This change has led many to view death as a tragedy rather than an integral transition. As we age, the weight of our mortality becomes heavier, prompting worries about our "drop dead date," a term that embodies the anxiety surrounding the end of life. This chapter aims to explore these shifting perspectives and how they influence our daily existence.

Historically, many cultures embraced death as a natural phase of the life cycle, celebrating it with rituals that honored the deceased and comforted the living. In stark contrast, modern society tends to marginalize death, pushing it to the periphery of our consciousness. This avoidance creates a paradox where, instead of living fully, we often find ourselves consumed by the fear of dying. The older we become, the more our thoughts can gravitate toward the finality of life, fostering a sense of urgency and anxiety about our remaining time. This shift in perspective can rob us of the joy and richness that life has to offer.

Yet, what if we could reframe our understanding of death?

Instead of viewing it solely as an ending, we might consider it a catalyst for living more intentionally. The awareness of our mortality can serve as a powerful motivator, encouraging us to prioritize what truly matters. By embracing the finite nature of our existence, we can cultivate deeper connections with loved ones and engage more fully with our passions. This perspective shift allows us to transform our fear into appreciation, prompting us to seize each moment instead of dwelling on the countdown.

Moreover, confronting our mortality can lead to profound personal growth. Acknowledging death can inspire us to reflect on our values, ambitions, and the legacy we wish to leave behind. This introspection often reveals what genuinely holds significance in our lives, urging us to align our actions with our core beliefs. As we face the reality of our mortality, we can shed the trivialities that often consume our attention, focusing instead on experiences that enrich our souls and foster meaningful relationships.

In the end, shifting our perspective on death from a source of dread to a catalyst for living fully can transform our existence. As we grapple with the knowledge that we are all waiting to die, we can choose to embrace life with vigor and purpose. By recognizing that every moment is precious, we can cultivate a mindset that honors our journey, allowing us to live authentically and deeply, regardless of the countdown that looms ahead.

Chapter 2: The Weight of Waiting

The Concept of Time

Time is an ever-present companion that shapes our lives in profound ways. From the moment we are born, we embark on a journey marked by the relentless ticking of a clock that serves as a constant reminder of our mortality. As we age, the weight of this awareness becomes heavier, and the concept of time transforms from a mere measurement to a poignant reflection of our existence. The notion that we are all waiting to die can feel disheartening, yet it also compels us to examine how we spend our days and the legacy we wish to leave behind.

In many ways, time is an illusion, a construct created by humans to impose structure on the chaos of existence. While we may divide our lives into years, months, and days, the essence of time is fluid and subjective. A moment can stretch indefinitely or pass in the blink of an eye, often determined by our emotional state or the experiences we encounter. As we confront our own mortality, we may find that our perception of time shifts dramatically. The past becomes a tapestry of memories, the present a fleeting opportunity, and the future a source of both hope and anxiety.

Acknowledging the finite nature of our lives invites us to consider what truly matters. In a society that often prioritizes productivity and achievement, the idea of living fully can seem elusive. We may chase after milestones, believing that reaching them will grant us a sense of fulfillment. However, as we grow older, we come to realize that the moments we cherish most are not those marked by accolades, but rather those filled with genuine connection, love, and joy. The awareness of our impending mortality serves as a catalyst for prioritizing these meaningful experiences over superficial pursuits.

As we navigate this journey, it becomes essential to cultivate mindfulness and presence. By anchoring ourselves in the present moment, we begin to appreciate the richness of our daily lives. Time, when viewed through the lens of mindfulness, transforms from a source of anxiety to a canvas upon which we can paint our experiences. Each day presents an opportunity to engage with the world around us, to express gratitude, and to forge connections that transcend the boundaries of time. In embracing the here and now, we can find solace in the knowledge that every moment is a gift, regardless of how fleeting it may be.

Ultimately, the concept of time is a reminder of both our fragility and our resilience. While the reality of waiting to die may evoke sadness, it also encourages us to live with intention and purpose. By reflecting on our relationship with time, we can shift our focus from fear of the inevitable to an appreciation of the journey itself. In doing so, we empower ourselves to create a life filled with meaning, connection, and joy—a life that honors our existence while we await the unknown.

Living in Limbo

Living in limbo is a state many of us find ourselves in as we navigate the complexities of life and the inevitable reality of death. It is a space filled with uncertainty, where the ticking clock serves as a constant reminder of our mortality. The older we get, the more pronounced this limbo becomes, as we often find ourselves reflecting on our lives, our choices, and the time we have left. This waiting period can feel heavy, almost suffocating, as we grapple with the fear of the unknown and the countdown that looms ahead.

In this existential waiting room, we may become preoccupied with thoughts about what we have accomplished and what remains undone. Regrets can surface, overshadowing the joy of the present. It is easy to fall into a cycle of worry and anxiety, fixating on the things we should have done differently or the dreams that seem out of reach. This mindset can rob us of the beauty that life still holds, as we allow the fear of death to dictate our experiences and diminish our sense of purpose.

Yet, living in limbo does not have to be solely about dread or despair. It can also serve as a powerful catalyst for reflection and growth. Acknowledging our mortality can inspire us to live with intention, to seek out meaningful connections, and to pursue passions that ignite our spirit. The awareness of time's fleeting nature can compel us to prioritize what truly matters, encouraging us to embrace each moment fully and to cultivate gratitude for the life we have, despite its inevitable end.

As we navigate this limbo, it is essential to seek support and connection with others who share our fears and uncertainties. Conversations about death and dying may feel uncomfortable, but they can also be profoundly liberating. By discussing our thoughts and feelings, we can demystify death and foster a sense of community. In doing so, we create a space where we can explore our vulnerabilities, share our stories, and ultimately find solace in the shared human experience of waiting.

Ultimately, living in limbo is an invitation to confront our fears rather than shy away from them. It challenges us to redefine our relationship with time, urging us to shift our focus from the end to the journey. By embracing the uncertainty that life presents, we can discover a deeper appreciation for the every day. It is within this liminal space that we can learn to live fully, not in spite of our mortality, but because of it, transforming the countdown into a celebration of life itself.

The Anxiety of Anticipation

The anxiety of anticipation often looms over us as we navigate the winding road of life. Each tick of the clock serves as a reminder of our mortality, instilling a sense of urgency that can be both motivating and paralyzing. For many, the awareness of our inevitable end can cloud the joy found in everyday moments. As we age, this awareness deepens, transforming into a constant companion that whispers reminders of our fragility. The anticipation of death can provoke a fear that shadows our daily experiences, making it difficult to embrace the present.

Living with the knowledge that our time is limited can evoke a range of emotions, from dread to reflection. We may find ourselves ruminating on unfulfilled dreams or unresolved relationships, and the weight of these thoughts can be overwhelming. Instead of engaging fully with life, we may retreat into our minds, replaying scenarios or worrying about what lies ahead. The very essence of anticipation can morph into a heavy burden, as we grapple with what our lives have meant thus far and what they may mean in the face of our mortality.

Yet, within this anxiety, there exists an opportunity for growth and understanding. Acknowledging our fears allows us to confront them, shifting our perspective from one of despair to acceptance. By recognizing that anxiety is a natural response to the unknown, we can cultivate a sense of resilience. This process of transformation invites us to explore how we can live more authentically, focusing on what truly matters to us in the limited time we have. Embracing our mortality can lead to a richer appreciation of life, encouraging us to prioritize meaningful connections and experiences.

The anticipation of death also serves as a powerful catalyst for change. It can inspire us to take risks, to pursue passions that we may have set aside, and to communicate openly with loved ones. As we confront the reality of our lives, we may feel compelled to engage in deep conversations about our fears and desires. This openness can foster stronger bonds and create a supportive environment where we feel safe to express our vulnerabilities. In this way, the anxiety of anticipation can be transformed into a force that propels us toward greater intimacy and understanding.

Ultimately, learning to navigate the anxiety of anticipation requires a delicate balance. It is essential to honor our feelings of fear while also seeking ways to engage with life fully. The journey toward acceptance is not linear; it is filled with moments of clarity and confusion. By acknowledging our shared human experience of waiting, we can find solace in the knowledge that we are not alone in our fears. In embracing this truth, we can learn to cherish the present, allowing ourselves to live fully and authentically, even as we confront the unseen countdown to our inevitable end.

Chapter 3: Finding Meaning in the Everyday

Mindfulness and Presence

Mindfulness and presence serve as vital tools in navigating the often daunting reality of mortality. In a world where we are perpetually aware of our finite time, the practice of mindfulness invites us to focus on the present moment, cultivating a deeper appreciation for the life we are living right now. As we confront the inevitability of death, it becomes crucial to engage with our current experiences fully, rather than allowing anxiety about the future to overshadow our daily existence. By embracing mindfulness, we can learn to savor each moment, transforming our awareness into a source of joy rather than a burden.

The act of being present requires deliberate effort, especially in a society that constantly pulls our attention in multiple directions. Our minds tend to dwell on regrets from the past or worries about the future, creating a mental landscape filled with anxiety. By practicing mindfulness, we can train ourselves to redirect our thoughts, anchoring them in the here and now. This shift allows us to experience life more vividly, whether it's enjoying the taste of our food, the warmth of the sun on our skin, or the laughter shared with loved ones. Through these simple yet profound moments, we can find meaning and beauty even amidst the awareness of our mortality.

Mindfulness also fosters a sense of acceptance regarding our inevitable fate. Rather than resisting the concept of death or allowing it to loom large in our minds, we can learn to accept it as a natural part of life. This acceptance does not diminish the gravity of our mortality but enhances our appreciation for the moments we have. When we acknowledge the transient nature of life, we can cultivate gratitude for each day we are given. This grateful mindset encourages us to live more fully, prompting us to engage in activities and relationships that truly matter.

Incorporating mindfulness into our daily routines can be as simple as setting aside a few minutes each day for reflection or meditation. These moments of stillness allow us to reconnect with ourselves and our surroundings, fostering a deeper understanding of our thoughts and feelings. As we practice being present, we may find that our worries about the future begin to dissipate, replaced by a sense of peace and clarity. This transformation can lead to a more fulfilling life, where we prioritize experiences that enrich our existence rather than those that merely distract us from our fears.

Ultimately, the journey of mindfulness and presence is not just about coping with the reality of death; it is about enriching the life we lead while we await our inevitable end. By cultivating awareness and appreciation for the present moment, we can diminish the weight of our anxieties and celebrate the fleeting beauty of life. Embracing mindfulness allows us to live authentically and meaningfully, transforming our perspective on mortality into one that inspires us to engage with life more profoundly. In recognizing that we are all waiting to die, we can choose to live fully, making each moment count.

The Beauty of Routine

Routine often carries a negative connotation, yet its beauty lies in the structure and comfort it provides amidst the uncertainty of life. As we navigate the ticking clock of mortality, embracing a routine can help us find clarity and purpose. The repetitive nature of daily activities can serve as a grounding force, reminding us that while the end is inevitable, the moments in between can be filled with meaning and joy. Each task, no matter how mundane, becomes a thread in the tapestry of our existence, offering a sense of normalcy in a world that often feels chaotic.

Within the framework of routine, we find a space to cultivate gratitude. The simple act of waking up at the same time each day, preparing a favorite breakfast, or taking a morning walk can transform our perspective. These rituals invite us to appreciate the small pleasures that life offers. Instead of solely focusing on the eventuality of death, we can shift our gaze to the beauty of being alive, even if it is for a fleeting moment. Each repetition becomes a reminder that life is composed of countless beautiful instances, and routine allows us to savor them fully.

Moreover, routines create opportunities for reflection. In our busy lives, it is easy to forget the importance of pausing and taking stock of where we are. By setting aside time for specific activities, such as journaling or meditation, we give ourselves permission to explore our thoughts and emotions. This intentional reflection can help us confront our fears about mortality, allowing us to process our feelings honestly. In doing so, we can shift from a place of anxiety to one of acceptance, embracing our mortality while finding peace in the present.

The beauty of routine also lies in its ability to foster connections with others. Whether it is a weekly family dinner or a regular coffee meetup with friends, these shared moments reinforce our bonds and remind us of the support systems we have in place. Routine can serve as a nurturing rhythm that not only enhances our personal lives but also strengthens our relationships. In times of uncertainty, the presence of loved ones during these familiar gatherings can be a source of comfort, helping us navigate the emotional landscape of waiting for the inevitable.

Ultimately, embracing routine does not mean we ignore the reality of our mortality. Instead, it offers a way to infuse our lives with purpose and joy as we wait. By finding beauty in the ordinary and allowing ourselves to engage with the present, we can create a fulfilling existence even in the shadow of death. Each day becomes a testament to our resilience, reminding us that while we may be waiting for an end, we are also living fully in the moments that define our journey.

Celebrating Small Moments

In the journey of life, we often find ourselves preoccupied with the grand milestones: birthdays, weddings, career achievements, and significant anniversaries. While these moments hold their importance, it is the small, seemingly insignificant moments that often escape our attention yet contribute profoundly to our overall experience. Celebrating these small moments allows us to cultivate a sense of gratitude and appreciation for the present, reminding us that life is not solely defined by its monumental events but rather by the accumulation of fleeting instances that bring us joy.

Consider the warmth of a morning cup of coffee, the laughter shared with a friend over a simple meal, or the serenity of a quiet evening walk. Each of these moments, while small in isolation, carries with it the potential for deep reflection and connection. They serve as gentle reminders that even amidst the uncertainty of life and the inevitable approach of our mortality, there is beauty to be found in the everyday. By consciously acknowledging and celebrating these small instances, we create a richer tapestry of experiences that can provide solace and joy, even during the most challenging times.

Moreover, recognizing and savoring these small moments can significantly shift our perspective on life. When we focus on the simple pleasures and everyday achievements, we begin to see life's value not just in what lies ahead, but in what is happening right now. This shift fosters a deeper appreciation for our surroundings, our relationships, and the very act of being alive. It encourages mindfulness, allowing us to fully engage with the present rather than being consumed by worries about the future. In a world that often seems to rush by, slowing down to celebrate the small moments can be a radical act of self-care.

As we navigate our daily lives, it's essential to create rituals around these small moments. Whether it's taking a moment to breathe deeply before starting the day, journaling about a pleasant interaction, or simply pausing to admire a sunset, these practices can help us anchor our awareness in the present. By intentionally celebrating the small victories and joys, we not only enhance our own well-being but also inspire those around us to do the same. This communal recognition of life's subtleties can foster a culture of appreciation and gratitude, reminding us that we are all in this together, facing the same uncertainties.

Ultimately, embracing and celebrating small moments is an act of defiance against the fear of our mortality. It is a way to reclaim our power and find meaning in our existence, regardless of how fleeting it may be. In acknowledging that life is a series of small, precious moments, we learn to cherish the time we have, fostering deeper connections with ourselves and others. As we navigate the unseen countdown, let us remember to pause, reflect, and celebrate the small moments that make life not just bearable, but profoundly beautiful.

Chapter 4: The Role of Relationships

Connection and Community

Connection and community are fundamental aspects of the human experience, yet they often become overshadowed by the looming reality of mortality. As we navigate the complexities of life, the awareness of our finite existence can lead us to withdraw, fostering isolation rather than connection. However, it is precisely in these moments of vulnerability that the bonds we form with others can provide a sense of solace. Embracing the reality of our mortality can serve as a catalyst for deeper relationships, encouraging us to seek out meaningful connections that enrich our lives.

In a world where the clock seems to tick louder as we age, we may find ourselves reflecting on the relationships that matter most. The fear of death can prompt us to reach out to loved ones, to express our feelings, and to forge new connections. These interactions can foster a sense of belonging and purpose, reminding us that we are not alone in our journey. By sharing our fears, hopes, and experiences with one another, we create a tapestry of support that can help alleviate the weight of our existential concerns.

Community plays a crucial role in shaping our perceptions of life and death. When we come together to share our stories, we begin to understand that we all share similar fears and longings. This collective wisdom can be incredibly healing. Engaging with others who are also contemplating their mortality can lead to profound discussions, offering insights that challenge our individual anxieties. In these spaces, we are reminded that life is not just about the inevitable end, but about the connections we cultivate along the way.

Participating in community activities, whether through organized groups or informal gatherings, can be a powerful antidote to the isolation that often accompanies thoughts of death. These interactions can range from volunteer opportunities to social clubs, each providing a platform for connection. When we engage with others, we create shared experiences that illuminate the beauty of life, encouraging us to focus on the present rather than dwelling on the future. This shift in perspective can transform our relationship with mortality, allowing us to embrace the journey rather than fear the destination.

Ultimately, the connections we nurture and the communities we build serve as reminders that life is a shared experience. While the reality of death is an unavoidable aspect of our existence, it can also inspire us to live more fully. By prioritizing relationships and fostering community, we cultivate a sense of belonging that transcends our fears. In this interconnectedness, we find strength, purpose, and a renewed appreciation for the time we have, encouraging us to live in a way that honors both our lives and the lives of those we cherish.

Love as a Counter to Fear

In the midst of our inevitable mortality, the emotions we grapple with can often overshadow the beauty of our existence. Fear, particularly the fear of death, looms large in our lives, especially as we age. This fear can paralyze us, leading to a life spent in worry rather than in appreciation of the present. However, love emerges as a powerful counter to this fear. It serves as a reminder of our connections, our joys, and the richness of our experiences. Love doesn't eliminate fear, but it allows us to reframe it and find purpose beyond the ticking clock.

Love has a transformative power that can shift our perspective on death. When we focus on the relationships we cherish, the bonds we nurture, and the moments filled with joy, fear takes a backseat. It's in the laughter shared with friends, the compassion shown to strangers, and the warmth of family that we begin to recognize the fleeting nature of life as an invitation to fully engage rather than retreat. Each act of love, no matter how small, contributes to a tapestry of meaning that can overshadow the shadows of fear, reminding us that we are part of something larger than ourselves.

Moreover, love encourages vulnerability, which can be daunting but ultimately liberating. When we allow ourselves to love deeply, we open ourselves up to the full spectrum of human experience, including the risk of loss. Yet, it is precisely this vulnerability that can lead to growth and resilience. The fear of what we might lose becomes less daunting when viewed through the lens of love. Instead of avoiding relationships to sidestep potential heartbreak, we can embrace them as opportunities to create lasting memories that transcend our fears. The connections we forge can serve as a testament to our lives, illuminating our path even as we face the end.

As we navigate the complexities of love, we also learn that it is a shared experience. The act of loving and being loved fosters a sense of community, reminding us that we are not alone in our fears. In sharing our stories of love and loss, we find solace in the collective understanding of our human condition. This communal aspect of love provides a buffer against isolation, helping us to confront our mortality not in solitude but as part of a larger narrative. Together, we can support one another, creating a sense of belonging that diminishes the sting of fear.

Ultimately, love invites us to live fully in the face of mortality. It encourages us to savor each moment, to express gratitude for the people in our lives, and to engage with the world around us with an open heart. As we learn to prioritize love, we discover that our countdown to death can be reframed as a countdown to meaningful experiences. By embracing love, we gain the strength to confront our fears, transforming the way we approach our inevitable end. Instead of being overshadowed by anxiety, we can choose to fill our remaining days with love, connection, and a deep appreciation for the life we have been given.

Leaving a Legacy Through Others

Leaving a legacy through others is a profound way to confront the inevitability of death while enriching the lives of those around us. As we navigate the complexities of life, the awareness of our mortality often looms large. It can be tempting to focus solely on our own existence and the fleeting nature of time. However, by shifting our perspective to how we can influence others, we can find purpose and meaning in our lives that transcends our individual experiences. This legacy is not just about what we leave behind in material terms but also in the values, lessons, and inspirations we impart to others.

Each interaction we have is an opportunity to create a ripple effect that can reach far beyond our immediate circle. Consider the young people in our lives—children, grandchildren, or even mentees. Every moment spent sharing wisdom, stories, or simply offering support can ignite a spark within them. This spark can inspire them to pursue their passions, make positive choices, and perhaps, in turn, influence others in their journeys. By investing our time and energy into nurturing the potential of those around us, we are effectively creating a legacy that can flourish long after we are gone.

In the digital age, our legacies can also extend through the stories we share online, the knowledge we impart through various platforms, and the connections we foster. Social media can be a powerful tool for building communities that reflect our values and ideas. By engaging with others in meaningful conversations, we can inspire collective action and foster a sense of belonging. The impact of a heartfelt message or a shared experience can resonate deeply, creating a lasting influence that informs the lives of many, even those we may never meet.

Moreover, leaving a legacy through others often involves acts of service and kindness. Volunteering, mentoring, or simply offering a listening ear can profoundly affect someone's life trajectory. These acts, though they may seem small in the grand scheme of life, can uplift others and inspire them to carry forward the spirit of generosity and compassion. In these moments, we become beacons of hope and strength, reminding others that life is not solely about waiting for the end but about embracing the journey and lifting each other along the way.

Ultimately, as we confront our mortality, we must recognize the power we hold to shape the future through our relationships and actions. By focusing on how we can leave a legacy through others, we find solace in knowing that our lives have meaning beyond our individual existence. This approach not only alleviates the weight of our worries about the "drop dead date" but also enriches our lives and the lives of others. In embracing this interconnectedness, we can live fully and intentionally, knowing that our influence will endure long after we take our final breath.

Chapter 5: Confronting Our Fears

Understanding Fear of Death

Fear of death is a universal experience that transcends cultural boundaries and individual backgrounds. It often manifests as a profound anxiety, troubling the mind and heart as we confront our mortality. This fear can be particularly acute as we age, leading to a heightened sense of urgency to understand our lives and the inevitability of their end. In grappling with this fear, it is crucial to acknowledge that it stems from our instinct for survival and the unknown that death represents. Rather than shying away from these feelings, we must face them head-on to find peace in our existence.

As we become more aware of our mortality, many of us find ourselves reflecting on the life we have led and the legacy we will leave behind. The fear of death often compels us to evaluate our choices, relationships, and achievements. This introspection can be both a source of anxiety and a catalyst for positive change. In this phase of reflection, we may seek to mend broken relationships, pursue unfulfilled dreams, or engage more deeply with those we love. Understanding that our time is finite can inspire us to live more authentically and courageously, making the most of each moment.

Furthermore, the fear of death can lead to a sense of isolation. In our society, discussions about mortality are often avoided, leaving many individuals to confront their fears in silence. This isolation can exacerbate feelings of sadness and despair, making it even more challenging to navigate our anxieties. By openly discussing death and our fears surrounding it, we can foster a sense of community and support. Sharing our vulnerabilities allows us to connect with others who feel similarly, reminding us that we are not alone in our struggles.

It is also essential to recognize that fear of death can serve a functional purpose in our lives. It can motivate us to prioritize what truly matters, urging us to engage fully with our passions and relationships. By understanding this fear as a natural part of the human experience, we can reframe it as a guide rather than an adversary. Embracing the reality of our mortality encourages us to appreciate the present, cultivating a deeper sense of gratitude for each day we have.

Ultimately, understanding the fear of death is a journey that leads us toward greater self-awareness and acceptance. Acknowledging this fear allows us to confront it and, in turn, find ways to live more fully. As we navigate through our lives, we can learn to embrace the uncertainty of our existence, transforming our fear into a powerful motivator for a life well-lived. By facing death with honesty and courage, we create space for a richer, more meaningful experience as we await the inevitable.

Tools for Coping

In the quiet moments of reflection, we often confront the reality of our mortality. This awareness can be unsettling, but it also presents an opportunity to cultivate tools that can help us cope with the anxiety surrounding our inevitable end. Acknowledging that we are all in a perpetual state of waiting can lead to meaningful conversations about life, purpose, and fulfillment.

Embracing our shared experience can create a bond that alleviates the weight of isolation in facing our fears.

One effective tool for coping is mindfulness. By practicing mindfulness, we learn to ground ourselves in the present moment, shifting our focus away from worries about the future. This practice can take many forms, such as meditation, deep breathing exercises, or simply taking a moment to appreciate the beauty around us. Engaging in mindfulness allows us to experience life more fully, helping us to find joy in the ordinary moments that often pass us by unnoticed. In doing so, we can confront our fears with a sense of clarity and peace, rather than being consumed by them.

Another valuable tool is the cultivation of meaningful relationships. Sharing our thoughts and feelings with others can lighten the burden of our worries. By forming connections with friends, family, or even support groups, we create a network of understanding that can provide comfort during difficult times. These relationships remind us that we are not alone in our fears, and they offer a safe space for vulnerability. Nurturing these bonds encourages us to live authentically and to embrace the moments we have with those we care about.

Journaling is a powerful method for processing our thoughts and emotions related to death and dying. Writing allows us to articulate our fears, hopes, and regrets, serving as an outlet for the complex feelings that often accompany our contemplation of mortality. By putting pen to paper, we can clarify our thoughts, confront our worries, and even discover insights that we might not have recognized otherwise. This practice not only fosters self-reflection but also encourages us to set intentions for how we wish to live, ultimately making our time more meaningful.

Lastly, engaging in acts of service can provide a profound sense of purpose. Contributing to the well-being of others can shift our focus from our own fears to the impact we can have in the world. Whether through volunteer work, mentoring, or simply lending a helping hand to someone in need, these actions remind us of the interconnectedness of life. In giving, we receive a sense of fulfillment that can counterbalance the heaviness of our mortality. By embracing these tools for coping, we can navigate the unseen countdown with a spirit of resilience and hope, living fully as we wait for the inevitable.

Transforming Fear into Motivation

Fear has a way of creeping into our lives, especially as we grow older and become increasingly aware of our mortality. This awareness can often lead to a paralyzing dread, a constant reminder of the fragility of life. However, it is crucial to recognize that fear, when transformed, can serve as a powerful catalyst for motivation. Instead of allowing the anxiety about our inevitable end to consume us, we can harness it to inspire action, embrace opportunities, and live with intention.

When we confront our fears, we begin to understand that they can be reframed. The fear of dying is not just about the end of life; it can also highlight the preciousness of each moment we have. This realization can ignite a sense of urgency within us. We start to ask ourselves what truly matters and what we want to accomplish before our time runs out. By making peace with our fears, we can transform them into a driving force that propels us toward our goals, relationships, and dreams.

Motivation derived from fear can manifest in various forms. It may encourage us to pursue long-held passions that we had shelved due to self-doubt or external pressures. It can inspire us to reconnect with loved ones, mend broken relationships, or express our feelings openly. The ticking clock of life can act as a reminder that our time is limited, urging us to act now rather than later. This shift in perspective allows us to prioritize what is truly important, leading to a more fulfilling existence.

Moreover, transforming fear into motivation fosters resilience. Each time we face our fears and take a step beyond our comfort zone, we build a bank of experiences that reinforce our strength. This resilience not only helps us confront our fear of death but also prepares us to tackle other challenges that life may present. We learn that while we cannot control the inevitability of our mortality, we can control how we respond to it. This proactive stance cultivates a sense of empowerment, reminding us that we have the agency to shape our lives.

Ultimately, the journey of transforming fear into motivation is deeply personal and unique for each individual. It requires introspection and a willingness to confront uncomfortable truths about our lives. As we navigate this process, we may find that our fears, once daunting, become a source of inspiration. In embracing the reality of our mortality, we can choose to live more fully, cultivate meaningful connections, and leave a lasting legacy that transcends our time on this earth.

Chapter 6: The Pursuit of Happiness

Redefining Success

Redefining success in the context of our mortality challenges us to look beyond conventional metrics such as wealth, status, and achievement. For many, success has been defined by societal standards that prioritize tangible accomplishments and external validation. However, as we grapple with the reality of our finite existence, it becomes clear that these markers often fail to capture the essence of a fulfilling life. Instead, success can be reimagined as a journey toward inner peace, meaningful connections, and a genuine appreciation for the moments we experience.

In a world that constantly pressures us to chase after more—more money, more possessions, more accolades—it is easy to overlook the significance of simply being present. As we age, the awareness of our mortality can serve as a catalyst for profound reflection. This reflection encourages us to evaluate what truly matters. Relationships with family and friends, acts of kindness, and moments of joy become the true measures of success. By shifting our focus from external achievements to internal fulfillment, we can cultivate a life rich with purpose and connection.

The fear of the "drop dead date" often leads to anxiety and regret, overshadowing the beauty of our daily lives. This anxiety can be paralyzing, causing us to postpone happiness in favor of future goals that may never be realized. Redefining success involves embracing the present moment and recognizing that every day is an opportunity to live fully. It invites us to celebrate small victories, whether it's sharing a laugh with a loved one or savoring a quiet moment of solitude. Each of these experiences contributes to a life well-lived, reminding us that success is not a destination but a series of moments that shape our existence.

Moreover, redefining success can inspire us to engage in acts of service and compassion, fostering a sense of community and belonging. When we prioritize the well-being of others, we enrich our own lives in ways that are profoundly satisfying. Helping others can shift our perspective from a self-centered view to one that values interconnectedness. This shift not only enhances our understanding of success but also brings us closer to the realization that we are all in this together, navigating the same uncertainties and fears.

Ultimately, redefining success is about embracing our shared humanity and recognizing that life is not a race against time. As we confront the inevitability of death, we are given the unique gift of clarity—a chance to realign our values and pursue what truly brings us joy. By letting go of societal pressures and expectations, we create space for authentic living. In this space, we find that success is not defined by what we achieve, but by how deeply we connect with ourselves and others in the time we have.

Joy in the Journey

In the midst of life's inevitable march toward its conclusion, it is easy to become consumed by the anxiety surrounding our mortality. The dread of the unknown can overshadow the beauty of our daily experiences, causing us to overlook the simple joys that punctuate our existence. However, it is within these moments that we often find the essence of what it means to truly live. By embracing the journey rather than fixating solely on the destination, we can uncover a profound sense of joy that exists even amid the reality of our finite lives.

Every day presents us with opportunities to create meaningful memories, whether it's sharing laughter with friends, savoring a quiet moment with a cup of coffee, or witnessing the beauty of a sunset. These experiences remind us that life is not merely a countdown to an end, but a collection of moments that define our existence. Focusing on the present allows us to cultivate gratitude, shifting our perspective from one of dread to one of appreciation for the here and now. Each breath, each interaction, and each tiny victory contributes to the rich tapestry of our lives.

Moreover, the journey of life often teaches us invaluable lessons that can transform our outlook on death. The struggles we face, the relationships we build, and the passions we pursue all shape who we are. They provide context to our experiences and help us understand that our time is not merely a finite resource but a precious gift. Embracing this idea can instill a sense of purpose, encouraging us to live fully and authentically, rather than merely waiting for the inevitable. In this way, we can find joy in the very act of living.

Engaging with others on this journey can further enhance our experience. Shared stories, laughter, and even moments of vulnerability create connections that enrich our lives. These relationships not only provide companionship but also serve as reminders that we are not alone in our fears and uncertainties. By opening up to one another, we can transform our individual struggles into collective strength, discovering that joy is often found in community and shared experiences.

Ultimately, joy in the journey is about embracing life's complexities with an open heart. It invites us to recognize that while death is a certainty, it does not diminish the beauty of life. Instead, it challenges us to live more deeply and intentionally. By fostering a mindset that celebrates each moment, we can navigate our fears and uncertainties with grace, allowing us to savor the richness of life until the very end. This perspective not only alleviates the weight of our mortality but also inspires us to truly engage with the world around us, finding joy in every step we take along the way.

Cultivating Gratitude

Cultivating gratitude is a profound practice that can transform our perspective, especially as we navigate the inevitability of our mortality. In a world that often emphasizes what we lack, fostering a sense of gratitude invites us to recognize the abundance around us. Each day offers countless small gifts, from the warmth of a morning sun to the comforting presence of loved ones. This shift in focus can help counterbalance the anxiety that comes with aging and the awareness of our finite existence. By intentionally acknowledging these moments of joy, we create a mental space that allows us to embrace life more fully.

As we age, the weight of our mortality can lead to a cycle of fear and regret. It is easy to become consumed by what we have not accomplished or the time we feel slipping away. However, gratitude serves as an antidote to this despair. When we make a conscious effort to appreciate the present, we begin to untangle ourselves from the burden of our worries. Reflecting on the things we are grateful for can also help us celebrate the richness of our experiences, reminding us that life is not solely defined by its end, but by the meaningful moments we create along the way.

Gratitude encourages us to cultivate deeper connections with others, enhancing our relationships as we acknowledge the contributions of those around us. In recognizing the kindness and support we receive from family, friends, or even strangers, we foster a sense of community and belonging. This interconnectedness can be a powerful source of comfort, particularly when we confront our fears about death. Sharing our gratitude not only strengthens our bonds but also creates an environment where others feel valued and appreciated, leading to a more fulfilling existence for everyone involved.

Incorporating gratitude into our daily routines can be as simple as keeping a journal or taking a few moments each morning to reflect on what we appreciate. This practice does not require grand gestures; rather, it thrives in the small, often overlooked aspects of life. Whether it's a cup of coffee enjoyed in silence or a smile exchanged with a neighbor, these moments are vital reminders that life continues to offer beauty, even amidst uncertainty. Over time, this habitual recognition of gratitude can reshape our outlook, helping us to approach each day with a renewed sense of purpose and joy.

Ultimately, cultivating gratitude is not just about feeling good; it is about fostering resilience in the face of mortality. By training ourselves to focus on what we have rather than what we lack, we empower ourselves to live with intention and appreciation. As we face the inevitable conclusion of our lives, let us embrace gratitude as a guiding principle. In doing so, we can find solace in the journey, cherishing every moment until our time comes to an end, and celebrating the life we have lived.

Chapter 7: The Power of Reflection

Journaling for Clarity

Journaling for clarity serves as a powerful tool for individuals who grapple with the weight of mortality. In a world that often shies away from conversations about death, the act of putting pen to paper allows for a safe space to explore our innermost thoughts and fears. By engaging in this reflective practice, we can untangle the complex emotions surrounding our existence, giving voice to anxieties that often remain silent. Each entry becomes a testament to our journey, capturing the essence of our feelings as we navigate the inevitable reality that awaits us all.

As we age, the countdown to our final moments can intensify feelings of anxiety and dread. Journaling offers an antidote to this growing unease. It invites us to confront our thoughts directly rather than allowing them to swirl aimlessly in our minds. This process can illuminate the areas where we feel stuck or overwhelmed, leading to a clearer understanding of what truly matters. With each word, we can identify the sources of our fears and, in doing so, take a step towards reclaiming our power over them.

Moreover, writing about our experiences can foster gratitude for the present moment. When we acknowledge our mortality, we often find ourselves appreciating the little things we might otherwise overlook. Journaling can shift our focus from what we fear losing to what we cherish in our lives right now. By documenting the beauty found in everyday moments, we cultivate an awareness that life, even in its fragility, is filled with profound joy and connection. This practice transforms our perspective, encouraging us to savor each day as a gift rather than merely counting down the days.

In addition to fostering gratitude, journaling can also serve as a means of creating a legacy. As we confront the realities of our mortality, we may feel a desire to leave something behind—words of wisdom, reflections on our lives, or messages to loved ones. Through journaling, we can articulate our values, share our stories, and express our hopes for those we leave behind. This act of creation not only provides clarity for ourselves but also ensures that our voices continue to resonate even after we are gone. It becomes a bridge connecting our past, present, and future in a meaningful way.

Ultimately, journaling for clarity is not just about facing the unpleasant truth of mortality; it is about embracing life in all its complexities. By allowing ourselves to explore our fears and hopes on the page, we can navigate the unseen countdown with greater authenticity and purpose. Each entry is an invitation to reflect deeply on what it means to live fully, even as we acknowledge the certainty of our eventual departure. In this practice, we find strength, insight, and a renewed commitment to making the most of our time, however limited it may be.

Life Reviews

Life reviews are a profound and often transformative experience that can occur as we approach the later stages of our lives. They involve a deep reflection on our past, our choices, and the moments that have shaped us into who we are today. In the quiet moments of introspection, we find ourselves sifting through memories, both cherished and painful, understanding how they contribute to the tapestry of our existence. This process can be a powerful tool for making sense of our journey, illuminating the lessons learned, and providing clarity as we navigate the final chapters of our life.

For many, the act of reviewing one's life can stir a complex mix of emotions. Regrets may surface, reminding us of dreams left unfulfilled or relationships that faded away. Yet, alongside these regrets, there is often a sense of gratitude for the experiences that brought joy and connection. The duality of these emotions can be heavy, but it is within this acknowledgment that we may find peace. Embracing our past, with all its imperfections, allows us to honor our struggles and triumphs alike, leading to a deeper understanding of our own humanity.

As we reflect on our lives, we may also begin to recognize patterns in our behavior and choices. This awareness can lead to significant personal growth, encouraging us to let go of resentments or fears that no longer serve us. Life reviews can inspire a shift in perspective, prompting us to prioritize what truly matters. We often realize that love, compassion, and connection are far more valuable than material success. By embracing these insights, we can actively choose to cultivate relationships and experiences that enrich our remaining days, rather than remaining paralyzed by the fear of death.

Moreover, life reviews often serve as a catalyst for forgiveness—both of ourselves and others. Acknowledging the mistakes made along the way may open the door to healing, allowing us to release burdens we've carried for far too long. This process can be liberating, transforming our anxiety about the end into a celebration of our journey. In doing so, we pave the way for a more profound appreciation of life, turning our focus from the inevitable conclusion to the richness of each moment we still possess.

Ultimately, engaging in a life review is not merely a reflection on what has been but a guiding light for how we wish to live moving forward. As we confront the reality of our mortality, we can choose to live with intention and authenticity, making the most of the time we have left. By embracing this practice, we not only honor our past but also empower ourselves to create a meaningful legacy, one that transcends our fears and reminds us that every moment is a gift worthy of celebration.

Learning from the Past

As we navigate through life, the shadow of mortality looms ever larger, particularly as we age. This awareness can weigh heavily on us, often leading to an anxious preoccupation with the inevitable end. However, rather than succumbing to despair, we have the opportunity to learn from our past experiences. The lessons we gather from our journey can provide insights that not only enrich our lives but also help us redefine our relationship with death. By reflecting on our past, we can cultivate a deeper understanding of what it means to truly live.

Each moment we have lived contributes to our current perspective. The joys and sorrows, successes and failures, all weave together into a tapestry that illustrates our unique experience. In times of reflection, we can uncover patterns in our decisions and behaviors that have shaped us. This process can illuminate the importance of embracing life fully, rather than merely waiting for it to conclude. It is through this lens that we begin to see our finite nature as a catalyst for living more authentically and with purpose.

Moreover, learning from the past encourages us to prioritize what genuinely matters. The ticking clock reminds us of the importance of connection, love, and shared experiences. In our busy lives, it is easy to overlook these vital aspects, focusing instead on trivial pursuits that distract us from deeper fulfillment. By revisiting our history, we can identify the moments that brought us joy and contentment, allowing us to intentionally seek similar experiences in the present. This conscious effort to live in alignment with our values can transform our approach to life and death alike.

Additionally, our past can teach us resilience. The struggles we have faced often serve as powerful teachers, imparting wisdom that can guide us through present challenges. When we acknowledge the hardships we have overcome, we cultivate a sense of strength and determination. This resilience not only prepares us to confront our mortality but also empowers us to embrace each day with renewed vigor. By accepting that life is a series of peaks and valleys, we can better appreciate the beauty of our existence, even in the face of uncertainty.

Ultimately, learning from the past is an invitation to embrace the fleeting nature of life. While it is natural to fear death, it is equally vital to recognize that this awareness can spur us to live more fully. Each lesson learned, each cherished memory, adds richness to our lives and offers a roadmap for the future. By honoring our past, we can shift our focus from the sadness of waiting to die to the profound joy of living, fostering a spirit of gratitude that permeates every moment we have left.

Chapter 8: Creating a Life of Purpose

Identifying Core Values

Identifying core values is a deeply personal journey that requires introspection and honesty. In a world where the inevitability of death looms ever closer, understanding what truly matters to us becomes essential. Core values serve as our guiding principles, shaping our decisions and influencing our relationships. As we navigate the complexities of life, especially in the face of mortality, recognizing these values can provide clarity and purpose. It helps us focus on what is truly significant, rather than getting lost in the minutiae of daily existence.

To begin identifying core values, one must reflect on pivotal moments in life. These moments often reveal what we cherish most. Consider times of joy, pain, or profound insight. What were the common threads in those experiences? Perhaps it was the feeling of connection with loved ones, the pursuit of knowledge, or a commitment to service. By considering these instances, we can start to unearth the beliefs and ideals that resonate deeply within us. This process is not about what we think we should value but rather about what naturally emerges from our own lived experiences.

In addition to personal reflection, seeking feedback from trusted friends and family can illuminate our core values. Sometimes, those closest to us can see patterns in our behavior and choices that we may overlook. Engaging in open conversations about what matters most in life can lead to enlightening revelations. By understanding how others perceive our values and priorities, we can refine our own understanding and gain additional insights into our motivations and desires.

Once we have identified our core values, the next step is to evaluate how well our current lives align with them. This reflection can be uncomfortable but is essential for living authentically. Are we making choices that honor our values, or are we succumbing to societal pressures and expectations? It's crucial to assess our daily actions and long-term goals against our identified values. When we live in alignment with our core beliefs, we experience a profound sense of fulfillment, even amidst the uncertainty of life's finite nature.

Finally, embracing our core values empowers us to live with intention and passion. In recognizing what is truly important, we can prioritize our time and energy accordingly. This clarity allows us to cultivate relationships that enrich our lives, engage in activities that bring us joy, and pursue endeavors that resonate with our sense of purpose. While the countdown to our final moments may seem daunting, understanding and embracing our core values transforms this wait into an opportunity for meaningful living. In this way, we not only confront the reality of death but also celebrate the life we have, making every moment count.

Setting Meaningful Goals

Setting meaningful goals is crucial in navigating the inevitable reality of our mortality. As we grapple with the ticking clock that life presents, it becomes more apparent that our days are finite. This recognition can either paralyze us with fear or motivate us to embrace our existence more fully. Goals, when crafted thoughtfully, serve as guiding stars that illuminate our path, helping us to extract meaning from our time on this earth. They encourage us to focus on what truly matters, allowing us to live with intention amidst the uncertainty of our future.

To begin, it is essential to reflect on what holds significance in our lives. Goals should resonate deeply with our values and passions, steering us toward experiences that enrich our souls. It is easy to get caught up in societal expectations or the pursuit of success defined by external standards. Instead, take time to delve into your own heart and mind. What do you cherish most? Is it family, adventure, creativity, or perhaps personal growth? The answers to these questions will help in sculpting goals that are not only achievable but also fulfilling.

Once you have identified your core values, the next step is to translate them into actionable goals. This involves breaking down larger aspirations into smaller, manageable tasks. For instance, if your goal is to nurture relationships with loved ones, consider setting a goal to spend quality time each week with family or friends. These smaller steps create a sense of progress and accomplishment, reinforcing your commitment to living a meaningful life. Remember, the journey toward your goals is just as important as the destination; each moment spent in pursuit of what you value adds richness to your daily existence.

Additionally, it is vital to remain flexible in your goal-setting. Life's unpredictability can often throw us off course, and our plans may need to adapt as circumstances change. Embrace this fluidity; allow your goals to evolve as you gain new insights and experiences. This adaptability not only alleviates the pressure of rigid expectations but also opens the door to unforeseen opportunities for growth and fulfillment. By staying open to change, you can ensure that your goals continue to align with your evolving self.

Ultimately, setting meaningful goals is about cultivating a sense of purpose amid the reality of our mortality. It is a reminder that while we may all be waiting for the final chapter, we have the power to write the story of our lives in a way that honors our true selves. By focusing on what matters most and taking deliberate steps toward those aspirations, we can find joy and fulfillment even in the face of life's most daunting truths. In this way, our goals become not just markers of achievement, but profound expressions of our humanity, allowing us to live fully while we navigate the unseen countdown.

Aligning Actions with Intentions

Aligning actions with intentions is a profound endeavor, especially when we acknowledge the reality that life is finite. As we navigate the complexities of aging, it becomes increasingly crucial to reflect on how our daily choices resonate with our deeper values and desires. The knowledge of our mortality, often overshadowed by the routine of everyday life, can serve as a powerful motivator to ensure that our actions truly reflect what we hold dear. Each moment presents an opportunity to bridge the gap between what we intend to do and what we actually do, transforming our existence from a mere waiting period into a meaningful experience.

In our pursuit of alignment, it is essential to engage in introspection. This process involves not just contemplating our goals but also recognizing the underlying intentions that drive them. When we examine our motives, we uncover what truly matters to us. Are we chasing achievements for external validation, or are we seeking fulfillment and connection? By clarifying our intentions, we can craft a path that honors our authentic selves. This alignment allows us to live with purpose, making choices that resonate with our true values rather than merely going through the motions.

However, aligning actions with intentions is not always straightforward. The pressures of societal expectations, personal fears, and habitual patterns can easily derail our efforts. It's easy to get caught up in the busyness of life, losing sight of what we originally intended. To counter this, we must cultivate mindfulness—an awareness of the present moment that enables us to pause and evaluate our actions. Mindfulness helps us to approach each decision with intention, allowing us to assess whether our current trajectory aligns with our deeper aspirations. Through this practice, we can gradually shift our lives from reactive patterns to conscious choices that reflect our true selves.

Moreover, accountability plays a vital role in this alignment process. Sharing our intentions with trusted friends or mentors can create a support system that encourages us to stay true to our goals. When we vocalize our aspirations, we invite others to hold us accountable, fostering an environment where we can discuss our struggles and celebrate our successes. This communal aspect of alignment reminds us that we are not alone in our journey, and it reinforces our commitment to live meaningfully as we await the inevitable.

Ultimately, aligning our actions with our intentions is about embracing the reality of our mortality with grace and authenticity. As we become more aware of our finite existence, we gain the clarity needed to prioritize what truly matters. By taking meaningful steps towards alignment, we transform the waiting period into a vibrant, fulfilling experience. This conscious effort to live fully, despite the ticking clock, allows us to approach life not with fear, but with gratitude for the moments we have and the connections we make along the way.

Chapter 9: The Art of Letting Go

Accepting Loss

Accepting loss is a journey that many of us traverse, often without realizing it until we find ourselves in the depths of grief or the shadows of anxiety. As we age, the reality of our mortality becomes increasingly apparent, and with it, a cascade of fears surrounding the inevitable end. This awareness can be overwhelming, prompting us to grapple with the losses we have experienced and those that lie ahead. The process of accepting loss is not just about acknowledging death; it is about understanding the value of what we have and allowing ourselves to grieve not only for what we have lost but also for what we may never have.

In this landscape of acceptance, we often encounter the stark reminder that loss is an intrinsic part of life. Whether it is the death of a loved one, the fading of dreams, or even the gradual decline of our own bodies, we are constantly faced with the reality that nothing is permanent. The older we grow, the more these losses accumulate, and the weight of them can feel unbearable. However, it is through the acceptance of these losses that we begin to find a deeper appreciation for the moments we still hold dear. Embracing this truth allows us to live more fully, as we learn to cherish our relationships and experiences, knowing that they are fleeting.

The act of surrendering to loss is often accompanied by a profound sense of vulnerability. It requires us to confront our fears head-on, acknowledging the pain that loss brings while also recognizing the beauty that can arise from it. As we allow ourselves to grieve, we create space for healing and growth. This process can be uncomfortable and challenging, yet it ultimately leads us to a place of greater understanding and compassion for ourselves and others. We discover that loss does not define us; rather, it shapes our perspectives and enriches our lives in unexpected ways.

As we navigate the terrain of loss, we also learn the importance of connection. Sharing our experiences, fears, and sorrows with others can be a powerful antidote to the isolation that often accompanies grief. In these moments of vulnerability, we find solace in knowing we are not alone in our struggles. The act of reaching out can foster empathy and understanding, creating a supportive network where we can collectively process our losses and celebrate the lives we still have. This shared journey not only helps us accept our own losses but also encourages us to honor the memories of those who have touched our lives.

Ultimately, accepting loss is a vital aspect of living fully while we wait to die. It reminds us that life is a precious gift, often taken for granted amidst the chaos of our daily routines. By embracing the reality of loss, we can cultivate a deeper sense of gratitude for every moment, every relationship, and every experience. In doing so, we transform our understanding of death from a source of fear to a catalyst for living authentically. As we learn to accept loss, we gain the wisdom to navigate our lives with grace, knowing that each day is an opportunity to love, to connect, and to truly be present in our journey.

Releasing Regrets

Releasing regrets is a crucial step in the journey toward living fully, especially as we confront the inevitability of our mortality.

Many of us carry the weight of unfulfilled dreams, missed opportunities, and words left unsaid, which can cast a shadow over our daily lives. These regrets often manifest as a persistent nagging in our minds, reminding us of what could have been. To truly embrace the present, we must learn to let go of the past and make peace with our choices. Understanding that regrets are a part of the human experience can help us shift our perspective and focus on what truly matters.

As we age, the urgency to confront our regrets intensifies. Each year that passes serves as a reminder of the time we have left, leading to a heightened awareness of our mortality. This awareness can be daunting, but it can also act as a catalyst for change. Embracing the idea that life is finite encourages us to take stock of our regrets and confront them head-on. By acknowledging our past decisions and the emotions tied to them, we can begin to process our feelings and find closure. This process is not about blaming ourselves but rather about understanding our growth and the lessons learned along the way.

Letting go of regrets requires a conscious effort and a willingness to forgive ourselves. This may involve reflecting on the choices we've made and recognizing that they were often based on the information and circumstances we had at the time. We must remind ourselves that everyone makes mistakes and that these experiences contribute to our unique narratives. Practicing self-compassion allows us to release the guilt and shame associated with our regrets, freeing us to focus on the present and the future. It is essential to embrace the idea that we are all imperfect beings navigating the complexities of life.

Engaging in conversations about our regrets can also be a transformative experience. Sharing our feelings with trusted friends or family members can foster connection and understanding, helping us feel less isolated in our struggles. These discussions can lead to insights and perspectives that we may not have considered on our own. Additionally, expressing our regrets in writing or art can be a powerful outlet, allowing us to externalize our feelings and gain clarity. By bringing our regrets into the open, we can begin to dismantle their hold on us and find a sense of liberation.

Ultimately, releasing regrets is about reclaiming our lives in the face of uncertainty. As we navigate the countdown of our existence, we can choose to focus on the present with gratitude and intention. By letting go of what weighs us down, we create space for new experiences, connections, and joys. This journey toward acceptance and release is not always easy, but it is essential for living fully while we wait. By embracing this process, we can transform our regrets into stepping stones toward a more fulfilling life, one that honors both our past and our potential.

Finding Freedom in Acceptance

Finding freedom in acceptance is a profound journey that many of us embark upon, often unconsciously. The weight of mortality looms over us, especially as we age, bringing with it an array of anxieties and fears. Yet, within the acceptance of our finite existence lies a paradoxical liberation. We often grapple with the idea that acknowledging our mortality is a surrender, but in reality, it is an empowering act. Accepting that we are all on borrowed time allows us to shift our focus from the fear of the inevitable to the richness of the moments we still have.

As we confront our mortality, it becomes clear that the worry about our "drop dead date" can consume us, overshadowing the joys of the present. We spend so much energy pondering what we cannot control that we neglect the beauty of living fully in the now. Acceptance invites us to step out of this cycle of worry and into a space where we can appreciate life as it unfolds. This shift in perspective doesn't diminish the reality of death; instead, it enhances our appreciation for life, encouraging us to cherish relationships, experiences, and the simple pleasures that often go unnoticed.

In our pursuit of acceptance, we can find solace in vulnerability. Sharing our fears and concerns with others who share similar anxieties fosters a connection that is both healing and transformative. When we articulate our worries about death and dying, we often discover that we are not alone in our feelings. This communal acknowledgment can dissolve the isolation that frequently accompanies our thoughts on mortality. Through open dialogues, we cultivate a sense of understanding and empathy, allowing acceptance to blossom and take root in our hearts.

Moreover, acceptance encourages us to redefine our priorities. Instead of living in the shadows of what could happen, we begin to focus on what truly matters. We learn to say yes to experiences that enrich our lives and to let go of trivial pursuits that drain our energy. The freedom found in this acceptance fosters a more authentic existence, empowering us to make choices that align with our values and passions. As we embrace our limitations, we also embrace the possibility of a more fulfilling life, one that celebrates the time we have rather than mourning what is to come.

Ultimately, finding freedom in acceptance is not about resigning ourselves to fate; it is about embracing our journey with all its imperfections. Acknowledging our mortality can be a catalyst for action, prompting us to live with intention and purpose. The freedom that comes from acceptance allows us to cast aside the shackles of fear and engage with life in a more meaningful way. As we navigate the unseen countdown, we can transform our anxiety into gratitude, finding peace in the knowledge that each moment is a gift to be cherished.

Chapter 10: Living Fully in the Moment

The Importance of Now

In the quiet moments of our lives, the weight of mortality often presses down on us, reminding us that time is a fleeting resource. We become acutely aware of the ticking clock, each second pulling us closer to the inevitable end. This awareness can lead to a pervasive sense of dread, particularly as we age. However, it is precisely this understanding of our limited time that can ignite a profound appreciation for the present moment. The importance of now lies in its ability to shift our perspective from fear of the unknown to gratitude for the experiences we still have the power to create.

Embracing the present means recognizing that while we cannot change the past or predict the future, we can influence our current reality. Each day offers a blank canvas, an opportunity to engage with life in meaningful ways. By focusing on the now, we cultivate a mindset that values each moment, transforming the mundane into the extraordinary. This shift in focus can help us break free from the shackles of anxiety that come with contemplating our mortality, allowing us to find joy in the simple act of being alive.

Moreover, living fully in the present encourages deeper connections with others. When we are fully engaged in the moment, we can listen more attentively, empathize more profoundly, and share our authentic selves without the cloud of worry. These genuine interactions not only enrich our lives but also create lasting memories that can sustain us through difficult times. The relationships we foster in the now become a source of strength and comfort as we navigate the uncertainties of life and death.

It is essential to acknowledge the fears that accompany the awareness of our mortality. Many individuals resort to avoidance as a coping mechanism, allowing worries about the future to overshadow their ability to live fully. However, by confronting these fears and accepting our shared human condition, we can find freedom in the present. The importance of now is amplified when we recognize that it is our only guarantee. Rather than allowing fear to dictate our choices, we can choose to embrace life with vigor and intention, making the most of our time.

Ultimately, understanding the importance of now serves as a catalyst for personal growth and fulfillment. It invites us to reflect on our priorities, encouraging us to pursue passions and dreams that may have been sidelined by the distractions of everyday life. By recognizing the fleeting nature of our existence, we are propelled toward living authentically, fostering a sense of purpose that transcends the inevitability of death. In this way, the present moment becomes not just a point in time but a vital part of our journey, urging us to live fully while we wait.

Engaging with Life

Engaging with life is a profound journey that invites us to confront the reality of our mortality while simultaneously embracing the richness of our existence. As we age, the awareness of our finite time can often overshadow the beauty that life offers. It is crucial to shift our perspective from one of waiting for the inevitable end to actively participating in the moments that define our journey. This engagement is not merely about filling our days with activities but about immersing ourselves in experiences that resonate deeply with our values and passions.

The fear of death can easily become a heavy weight, pressing down on our spirits and stifling our enthusiasm for life. However, acknowledging this fear can serve as a catalyst for change. By recognizing that our time is limited, we can cultivate a sense of urgency that propels us to seek meaningful connections, pursue long-held dreams, and savor the fleeting joys that each day brings. Engaging with life means making conscious choices to prioritize what truly matters, allowing us to live not in the shadow of our mortality but in the light of our potential.

One effective way to engage with life is through the practice of mindfulness. This involves being fully present in each moment, appreciating the sights, sounds, and sensations around us. Mindfulness encourages us to slow down and take stock of our feelings, fostering a deeper connection with ourselves and the world. By embracing this practice, we can transform mundane routines into opportunities for reflection and gratitude, turning our focus away from the countdown and toward the richness of everyday experiences.

Engagement also requires us to cultivate relationships that nourish our souls. In a world that often emphasizes individualism, it is essential to seek out connections with others who inspire and uplift us. Whether through family, friends, or community, these bonds can offer support and joy, reminding us that we are not alone in our journey. Sharing our stories, fears, and dreams with others can create a tapestry of understanding and love, enriching our lives and deepening our sense of belonging.

Ultimately, engaging with life is about embracing both the beauty and the fragility of our existence. It invites us to live with intention, to make choices that reflect our values, and to celebrate each moment as a precious gift. As we confront the reality of our mortality, let us not succumb to despair but rather rise to the challenge of living fully. By doing so, we can transform our wait into a vibrant experience, finding meaning and joy even as we navigate the unknown.

Making Every Day Count

In the quiet moments of our lives, we often find ourselves grappling with the reality of mortality. Each passing day serves as a reminder that our time is finite, and this awareness can cast a long shadow over our existence. However, rather than allowing this knowledge to weigh us down, we can choose to view it as an invitation to truly engage with the present. Making every day count is not merely a motivational mantra; it is a profound commitment to embracing life in all its complexities, joys, and challenges.

To make every day count, we must first cultivate an understanding of what it means to live intentionally. This involves reflecting on our values, passions, and the relationships that nourish our souls. When we take the time to identify what truly matters to us, we can align our daily actions with these core principles. It is in these moments of clarity that we can break free from the mundane routines that often cloud our perception of time. A simple act of gratitude or a heartfelt conversation can transform an ordinary day into a cherished memory, reinforcing the idea that life is not measured solely by milestones but by the richness of our experiences.

As we navigate the complexities of aging and the accompanying anxieties about our mortality, it is essential to foster a mindset that embraces the beauty of impermanence. Each day offers us new opportunities to create meaning and connection, and by recognizing the fleeting nature of time, we can learn to appreciate each moment more deeply. This shift in perspective encourages us to prioritize our well-being—physically, emotionally, and spiritually. Engaging in activities that bring us joy, nurturing our relationships, and investing in self-care can all contribute to a more fulfilling daily existence.

Moreover, making every day count requires us to confront our fears about death and the unknown. Acknowledging our worries can be liberating, as it allows us to focus on the life we have rather than the life we fear losing. By sharing our thoughts with others, we can foster a sense of community and support, reminding ourselves that we are not alone in our struggles. This collective vulnerability can lead to deeper connections and a shared commitment to living fully, despite the uncertainties that lie ahead.

Ultimately, the act of making every day count is a personal journey that invites us to redefine our relationships with time and existence. It encourages us to savor the present, to find joy in the small moments, and to leave behind a legacy of love and connection. As we embrace the reality of waiting for our final days, let us commit to living with intention, fostering resilience, and celebrating the beauty of life in all its forms. In doing so, we can transform the weight of our mortality into a powerful catalyst for a life well-lived.

Chapter 11: Preparing for the End

Conversations About Death

Conversations about death often evoke a range of emotions, from fear to indifference, and yet, they are a natural part of our human experience. As we age, the reality of our mortality becomes increasingly pronounced, casting a shadow over our daily lives. This acknowledgment can feel heavy, yet it also opens the door to deeply meaningful discussions. Engaging in these conversations can provide a sense of relief, allowing us to confront our fears and uncertainties about what lies ahead, rather than letting them linger silently in our minds.

Discussing death is not merely about the end; it is also an opportunity to reflect on the life we have lived and the legacy we wish to leave behind. These conversations serve as a reminder that life is precious and fleeting. By sharing our thoughts and feelings about death with loved ones, we can celebrate the moments that have shaped us. Such discussions can bring families closer, fostering a sense of connection and understanding that transcends the inevitable separation that death brings. It encourages us to cherish our time together and to be intentional in our relationships.

Cultural attitudes toward death significantly influence how we approach these conversations. In many cultures, death is a taboo subject, often shrouded in silence and fear. This stigma can perpetuate feelings of isolation and anxiety for those grappling with the reality of mortality. By breaking down these barriers, we can create a space where open dialogue is not only accepted but encouraged. This shift can empower individuals to voice their concerns, hopes, and fears, helping to demystify death and alleviate the loneliness that often accompanies it.

Moreover, discussing death can lead to practical considerations that enhance our quality of life. Conversations about end-of-life wishes, funeral plans, and even the distribution of belongings can ease the burden on our loved ones during an already difficult time. When we proactively address these topics, we not only alleviate stress for ourselves but also provide clarity and direction for those we leave behind. This foresight can foster a sense of peace, knowing that we have taken steps to ensure our wishes are honored and that our loved ones are supported in their grief.

Ultimately, conversations about death can serve as a catalyst for living more fully. By embracing the reality of our mortality, we are reminded of the importance of each moment. These discussions encourage us to live with intention, pursue our passions, and strengthen our connections with others. In a world where the countdown to death is a shared experience, acknowledging this truth can transform our perspectives, allowing us to appreciate the beauty of life even in the face of its inevitable end.

Practical Considerations

In the journey of life, we often find ourselves grappling with the inevitability of death, a reality that becomes increasingly palpable as we age. This awareness can cast a long shadow over our daily existence, leading to a preoccupation with our mortality. However, rather than allowing this knowledge to paralyze us with fear, it can serve as a powerful catalyst for living more fully. Acknowledging our shared experience of waiting for the inevitable can foster a sense of connection with others, encouraging us to embrace the fleeting moments of joy and beauty that life offers.

One of the practical considerations in this context is the importance of cultivating meaningful relationships. As we confront the reality of our mortality, we often realize that the bonds we share with friends and family are what truly enrich our lives. Investing time and effort into nurturing these connections can create a support system that not only helps us cope with our fears but also enhances our overall quality of life. By prioritizing relationships, we can find solace in the shared human experience of both living and dying, transforming our perspective from one of isolation to one of community.

Another vital aspect is the need to engage in activities that promote a sense of purpose. Finding meaning in our daily lives can be a powerful antidote to the anxiety surrounding death. Whether through creative pursuits, volunteering, or pursuing lifelong passions, engaging in activities that resonate with our values can instill a sense of fulfillment. This not only distracts us from the fear of death but also enriches our lives, allowing us to leave a legacy that transcends our physical existence. By focusing on what brings us joy and a sense of accomplishment, we can shift our mindset from one of waiting to one of active participation in life.

Mindfulness and self-reflection also play crucial roles in navigating our thoughts about mortality. By developing a practice that encourages us to be present in the moment, we can alleviate some of the anxiety tied to our fears of death. Techniques such as meditation, journaling, or simply spending quiet time in nature can help us confront our feelings, allowing for a deeper understanding of our relationship with life and death. Through mindfulness, we can cultivate a sense of acceptance, recognizing that while death is inevitable, it does not diminish the value of our experiences or the beauty of our journey.

Ultimately, the practical considerations surrounding our awareness of mortality urge us to live with intention. Rather than waiting for the drop-dead date to dictate our actions, we can choose to embrace each day as an opportunity for growth, connection, and joy. By reshaping our mindset and taking actionable steps towards a fulfilling life, we can transform the fear of death into a motivating force that inspires us to live more authentically and passionately. In doing so, we not only honor our own existence but also contribute to a richer, more meaningful world for those around us.

Spiritual Perspectives on Death

Spiritual perspectives on death offer a lens through which we can examine our existence and the inevitability of our mortality. For many, death is often seen as a frightening endpoint, a dark void that looms over our lives. However, various spiritual traditions encourage us to reframe our understanding of death, viewing it not as a conclusion but as a transition into another state of being. This shift in perspective can alleviate some of the anxiety surrounding our inevitable departure from this world, allowing us to embrace life more fully in the present.

In many religious teachings, death is perceived as a gateway to a different realm, a journey rather than an end. For instance, in Hinduism, the belief in reincarnation suggests that each life is a chapter in a larger story, where the soul continues to evolve. This perspective can empower individuals to live with intention, focusing on their actions and choices. Rather than seeing death as a finality, it becomes an opportunity for growth and transformation, encouraging a deeper engagement with life's experiences.

Similarly, Buddhism offers profound insights into the nature of existence and impermanence. The concept of anatta, or non-self, teaches that clinging to the idea of a permanent self leads to suffering. By understanding that life is transient, we can cultivate a sense of peace regarding our mortality. This awareness encourages mindfulness, prompting us to appreciate each moment as it is, rather than being consumed by fears about the future. Embracing this perspective can lead to a more fulfilling existence, where we prioritize relationships, experiences, and personal growth over the anxiety of death.

Many spiritual traditions also emphasize the importance of connection and community in the face of death. Rituals surrounding death, such as memorial services and commemorative practices, serve to honor the deceased while also providing solace to the living. These communal expressions of grief and remembrance reinforce the idea that while our physical bodies may perish, the impact of our lives continues through the memories and love we share with others. This interconnectedness can provide comfort in the face of mortality, reminding us that we are not alone in our fears and uncertainties.

Ultimately, embracing a spiritual perspective on death can transform our relationship with life itself. By recognizing death as a natural part of existence, we can cultivate a greater appreciation for the time we have. This acknowledgment can inspire us to live more authentically, pursue our passions, and strengthen our connections with others. As we navigate the journey of life, understanding death as a transition rather than an end can empower us to make the most of our time, living fully while we wait for the inevitable.

Chapter 12: A Celebration of Life

Rituals and Memorials

Rituals and memorials serve as profound expressions of our shared humanity, especially as we navigate the inevitable reality of mortality. In a world where the countdown to our last breath looms ever closer, these practices allow us to acknowledge the fragility of life while also celebrating its beauty. They invite us to pause, reflect, and honor the lives we have lived and the connections we have forged. By engaging in such rituals, we can confront our fears and anxieties about death, transforming them into acts of remembrance and love.

The significance of rituals becomes even more apparent as we enter the later stages of life. For many, the act of commemorating a loved one provides a tangible way to process grief and loss. Funerals, memorial services, and personal ceremonies create spaces where we can gather with others who share our sorrow and celebrate the life that has passed. These events foster a sense of community, reminding us that we are not alone in our struggles. They serve as a powerful reminder that while death may separate us physically, our memories and shared experiences keep us connected.

In addition to the communal aspect of memorials, personal rituals can offer solace and comfort. Lightening candles, visiting cherished locations, or creating art in memory of those we have lost are just a few ways individuals can engage in meaningful practices. These acts allow us to express our feelings in a tangible form, providing an outlet for emotions that can often feel overwhelming. By carving out time for these rituals, we acknowledge our pain while also embracing the joy of the memories we carry with us.

Rituals and memorials can also serve as a catalyst for discussions about our own mortality. By reflecting on the lives of those who have passed, we are prompted to contemplate our own legacies and the impact we wish to leave behind. This introspection can lead to a deeper understanding of what it means to live fully. Engaging in conversations about death and dying, whether through formal gatherings or informal discussions, can help demystify the process and reduce the fear surrounding it. When we approach the topic with sincerity and openness, we create an environment where acceptance and understanding can flourish.

Ultimately, rituals and memorials remind us that while death is an inevitable part of life, it does not define our existence. Instead, they encourage us to celebrate the moments we have and to cherish the relationships that shape us. By participating in these practices, we not only honor those we have lost but also affirm our commitment to living authentically and fully in the time we have left. In doing so, we transform our awareness of mortality from a source of anxiety into a powerful motivator for connection, love, and purpose.

Honoring Our Stories

Honoring our stories is an essential act of recognition in a world where time often feels like an enemy. Each of us carries a unique narrative that shapes our existence, a tapestry woven with moments of joy, sorrow, triumph, and loss. As we face the inevitability of our mortality, it becomes increasingly vital to reflect on these stories, not only as a means of understanding our past but also as a way to enrich our present. By honoring our stories, we acknowledge the experiences that have brought us to this point, creating a sense of continuity and purpose even as we navigate the uncertainties of life.

In the hustle and bustle of daily living, it's easy to overlook the significance of our individual journeys. However, every story holds value, each one a testament to resilience and the human spirit. These narratives offer solace, reminding us that we are not alone in our struggles. When we share our stories, we connect with others, breaking down the barriers of isolation that can accompany the fear of death. This communal experience fosters empathy and understanding, allowing us to see ourselves in one another and appreciate the shared human condition.

As we age, the weight of our stories can feel heavier, often accompanied by regrets or unfulfilled desires. Yet, it is essential to transform this weight into a source of strength. By revisiting and reframing our narratives, we can find meaning in the trials we have faced. Each chapter of our lives contributes to who we are today, and recognizing the lessons learned along the way can empower us to live more fully. Embracing our pasts with compassion enables us to release the burdens that no longer serve us, leading to a more authentic existence.

Honoring our stories also invites us to celebrate our achievements, no matter how small. In a society that often prioritizes productivity and external validation, it can be easy to overlook the significance of personal milestones. Reflecting on our journeys allows us to acknowledge the courage it took to overcome obstacles and the joy found in simple moments. Celebrating these victories, both big and small, nourishes our spirits and instills a sense of hope and gratitude, reminding us that life is a precious gift, even in the face of its inevitable end.

Ultimately, honoring our stories is an invitation to live with intention as we await the unknown. It encourages us to embrace vulnerability, to share openly with others, and to reflect on the beauty of our existence. As we navigate the unseen countdown of our lives, let us commit to cherishing our narratives and those of others. In doing so, we cultivate a deeper appreciation for the time we have, transforming the fear of death into a celebration of life, rich with meaning and connection.

Living as a Tribute to Those We Love

Living as a tribute to those we love involves embracing the very essence of what it means to connect with others on a profound level. As we face the inevitability of our mortality, the memories and legacies of our loved ones guide us in navigating our own paths. Each moment spent honoring their lives can transform our outlook, shifting our focus from the fear of death to the richness of life. By living fully in their memory, we create a tapestry of shared experiences, reminding ourselves that love transcends the boundary of life and death.

To honor those we have lost, we can reflect on their qualities that inspired us. Perhaps it was their kindness, resilience, or passion for life that left an indelible mark on our hearts. By embodying these traits in our daily lives, we carry their spirit with us, ensuring that their influence continues to shape our actions and decisions. This practice not only strengthens our connection to them but also enriches our own existence. Each small act of kindness or courage becomes a living tribute, a testament to the impact they had on us.

In the face of our own mortality, we often find ourselves retreating into worry and anxiety about what lies ahead. Yet, when we choose to celebrate the lives of those we love, we cultivate a sense of gratitude for the time we have shared. This shift in perspective can be a powerful antidote to the fear of death. By acknowledging the beauty of our loved ones' lives, we can foster a sense of continuity, understanding that their legacy lives on through us. This realization can transform our waiting into a more meaningful journey, one filled with purpose and love.

Creating rituals or dedicating time to remember those we cherish can also serve as a profound tribute. Whether through storytelling, revisiting favorite places, or engaging in activities they loved, these actions allow us to celebrate their lives while simultaneously enriching our own. Each ritual acts as a bridge between the past and present, reminding us that our relationships do not end with death. Instead, they evolve, encouraging us to carry forward the lessons and love we have received.

Ultimately, living as a tribute to those we love is not just a way to cope with the reality of death; it's a celebration of life itself. It teaches us to embrace each moment, to find joy even in the face of sorrow, and to recognize the interconnectedness of our experiences. In doing so, we not only honor our loved ones but also inspire others to cherish their own relationships. By choosing to live fully, we affirm that love is a legacy that carries on, even in the quiet moments before we, too, reach the end of our own countdown.

About the Author

George Hatcher is a man who has always believed that the world is full of opportunities waiting for those bold enough to seize them. With a ninth-grade education and a wealth of unique experiences, he has faced the ups and downs of life head-on. At the age of 20, while serving time, George took the initiative to complete the assignments and tests necessary to earn his high school diploma. His own life is a treasure trove of stories waiting to be uncovered.

Over the years, George has enjoyed a diverse career as an entrepreneur, consultant, and strategist. He has served as a peacemaker for athletes and their parents, as well as a crisis management advisor for physicians and attorneys, achieving considerable success in client development and public relations. He is a licensed boxing manager in California, though he currently has no boxers signed.

George has logged over 200,000 air miles annually through business travel and pleasure trips with his wife. However, since the onset of COVID-19 in 2020, his travel has come to a halt. Now, in retirement, George finds that life remains an ongoing adventure. Unfortunately, he is fighting several new battles that he never anticipated, yet he continues to discover something new with each step.

As a passionate storyteller, George has published a dozen books and finds immense joy in writing. With the world opening up again, he has seized the opportunity to immerse himself fully in his literary pursuits. He currently resides in Rancho Mirage, California, with his wife, Molly, his partner for 59 years, and their home is filled with three cats and two macaws. Each experience in his life has taught him invaluable lessons about adaptability, perseverance, and a touch of luck. Like the person who hits their head just to feel the pleasure of stopping, George has made his share of mistakes—some more than once. He hopes others can learn from them as he has.

Now devoted entirely to writing, George Hatcher invites others to join him on this remarkable journey, filled with lessons and stories that showcase the beauty of life's unpredictability.

A longer bio is on his website at http://georgehatcher.com/bio/bio.html

www.ingramcontent.com/pod-product-compliance
Lightning Source LLC
Chambersburg PA
CBHW060704030426
42337CB00017B/2760